THE BETTER YOU

THE BETTER YOU
Knowledge, Understanding, & Preparation Are The Roots of Success

STEVEN BERRYHILL JR., Ph.D.

Published by SBJ LEADERSHIP, LLC
116 Agnes Rd
STE 200
Knoxville, TN 37919
www.sbjleadership.com

For ordering information, visit the author's website at: www.sbjleadership.com

Note to readers:
This publication is designed to provide accurate and authoritative information in regard to the subject matter covered. It is sold with the understanding that neither the author nor the publisher is engaged in rendering legal, investment, or accounting services. While the publisher and author have used their best efforts in preparing this book, they make no representations or warranties with respect to the accuracy or completeness of the contents of this book and specifically disclaim any implied warranties of merchantability or fitness for a particular purpose. The advice and strategies contained herein may not be suitable for your situation. Neither the publisher nor the author shall be in no way liable for any loss or damages.

Book cover design: Steven Berryhill Jr., Ph.D.

ISBN: 979-8-9912522-0-1

Printed in the United States of America

DEDICATION

This book is dedicated to my late father, Steven Brian Berryhill, who inspired me to live with purpose, achieve my goals, and live selflessly for others. I am forever grateful for his love, presence, support, and guidance throughout my entire life.

My father passed while I was working on this book. Very unexpectedly, I received a call one Saturday morning from my mother (Winford Felicia Berryhill) to return home to Georgia immediately. That was the worst phone call of my life. Distraught and flooded with emotions, I left Tennessee urgently and rushed to the hospital where my father was kept to experience the worst day of my life. During his last moments, I attempted to share with him something that I had not shared with anyone else at the time - that I was writing this book. Due to his medical state, I'm not even sure if he heard me tell him. I do however know that, although he would've been initially surprised to see that I wrote this book, he wouldn't have expected anything less from me. I also deeply know that he would've loved this book and been as immensely proud of me as my mother.

Thank you eternally "Pops" for being my foundation and giving me the tools that I needed to become the man I am today. You and Mom will always be my biggest source of love, guidance, motivation, and inspiration.

CONTENTS

FOREWORD

"Dr. Berryhill's new book *The Better You: Knowledge, Understanding, & Preparation are the Roots of Success* will help you find the inner strength you never knew you had. His book unlocked a multitude of positive things about myself that I wasn't previously aware of. This book is truly a guide to becoming a better version of yourself and is life-changing for people of all ages and from all walks of life."

- Tommie Mabry, Ph.D.
Best-Selling Author and Speaker

ACKNOWLEDGEMENTS

To my parents Steven and Winford Felicia Berryhill, thank you for your endless love, support, guidance, sacrifices, and patience. You will forever be my foundation, source of strength, and inspiration to succeed and help others. I thank God for being blessed with parents as great as you.

To Jaimie Glatt, thank you for your love, patience, and support throughout this beautiful journey. You are truly one of my biggest inspirations to become a better version of myself every day.

To Dr. Tommie Mabry, thank you for the constant inspiration, support, feedback, and motivation throughout this entire journey. You showed me how to turn my dream of becoming a published author into a reality.

INTRODUCTION

The Better You: Knowledge, Understanding, & Preparation are the Roots of Success is a transformative book that focuses on helping you to develop the mentality, tools, practices, and habits that lead to deep personal growth, increased goal accomplishment and success, and personal greatness. This book is strategically designed to reshape the way you think about growth and success by helping you to reframe the way you approach your vision and goals. A total of 25 gems are included to guide, elevate, motivate, and inspire you to walk in your purpose, reach your full potential, and expand your success.

Like the three parts of a tree (the roots, the trunk, and the crown), this book has been likewise divided into three parts of success - The Foundation of Manifestation & Success (The Roots), Working Towards Manifestation & Success (The Trunk), and Reaching & Keeping Success (The Crown). The three parts of this book are built on each other to help you fully develop and embody the necessary qualities of a successful person. Part I focuses on the foundational tools, understanding, and mentality you need to begin accomplishing your goals. Part II centers on expanding your foundational knowledge and tools to take your goals and ideas from inception to manifestation. Lastly, Part III focuses on the importance of developing an expansive mindset and sustainable habits as you begin to experience success.

Three sets of powerful affirmations, containing all 25 gems presented throughout the book, are provided at the end to help you align daily with your goals and intentions. Lastly, this book concludes with a dedicated reflection and planning section that allows you to use your gems to successfully plan for your future.

In every way, The Better You: Knowledge, Understanding, & Preparation are the Roots of Success will guide you to become a better version of yourself, help you to accomplish your goals and dreams, and motivate you to use your purpose to leave a positive mark on the world.

"There is no better time
to become a better you.
There is no better time
to start than now."

PART I

THE FOUNDATION OF MANIFESTATION & SUCCESS (THE ROOTS)

"THE STRONGER YOUR ROOTS, THE STRONGER YOUR LIKELIHOOD OF GROWTH AND SUCCESS."

MENTALITY

**"It all starts
in the mind."**

Mentality is everything. It's what separates those who are successful from those who are not, strength from weakness, opportunity from chance, and positive from negative outcomes, perspectives, actions, and experiences. The mentality you choose to have is extremely important because it has a deep effect on your entire life - for better or worse. Choosing to have a strong and high vibrational mentality is imperative for growth, evolution, and ascension to higher levels of being, understanding, manifestation, and success.

The world's most successful people tend to share several common traits, one being that they are mentally strong. People who are mentally strong take risks, go after what they want, and aren't afraid to fail. In fact, they fail quite often. To mentally strong people, failure is nothing more than an opportunity to learn, grow, and become wiser. These types of people have a deep hunger to succeed, let absolutely nothing get in the way of their success, and tend to be very competitive. Whether they're competing with others in their fields, or simply their reflection in the mirror, mentally strong and successful people possess an unquenchable thirst to better themselves every day.

In a deeper sense, being mentally strong is about being able to cope with and manage unfavorable circumstances, pressures, challenges, doubt, or failures. These moments are completely normal and are the times where your mental strength and faith are tested the most. Having the mentality to push through these challenging times is critical for your development and character and is pivotal to your future outcomes in life.

Most people never develop a strong mentality because they lack confidence, vision, and discipline. If you want to accomplish your goals and elevate your life, you have to commit yourself to your goals every day, have confidence in your vision, and get the work done no matter what. A strong mentality is rooted in hard work, working smart, focus, discipline, confidence, and patience. Operating on this powerful mental frequency gives you the ability to accomplish virtually anything you desire because, by its nature, you are operating in a state of attraction and manifestation. On this frequency, deep change and growth begins to happen rapidly in your life.

Fortunately, a strong mentality is something that can be learned and developed over time. Developing a strong mentality is the result of multiple factors, including having a strong sense of self and confidence in your abilities. It is also the direct result of the pattern of your mindset (a more fluid state of your mind regarding your attitudes and beliefs). Overall, a strong mentality develops when you allow experience to teach you the power of being focused, brave, confident, knowledgeable, faithful, and tenacious in your pursuits. It is earned when you transcend your fears and maintain the belief that nothing can stop or prevent you from accomplishing your goals. This type of mentality, the mentality to withstand and overcome obstacles of any form, is something that most people in this world don't have and why only such a small percentage of people become great. It is the mentality of your higher self; the you that demands greatness and refuses to settle for anything less, especially your own lower state of being.

Mentality is your first gem! It is the genesis of becoming a better you, through which all things are possible. Change your mentality and your life will change. Every chance you get, remind yourself that you are great and that you can accomplish whatever you want. Believe that you are powerful and well on your way to accomplishing your goals to elevate your life. Never become lazy or complacent, rely on status or luck, or throw in the towel at any point. Instead, passionately try to become a better version of yourself every day and keep going. That is the mentality of a winner and of someone who will obtain success and become great.

NOTES

NOTES

ENVIRONMENT

"A tree in the wrong environment never survives."

Just like your mentality, your environment can also make or break your success. Your environment can either provide you with the proper resources, foundation, and support you need to succeed, or it can create hardship, stress, trauma, and destruction in your life. Whether positive or negative, your environment certainly impacts you in some way shape or form and plays a role in your development, outlook, and outcomes in life. Since you are a direct product of your immediate environment, it is vastly important to dwell amongst people, places, and things that are conducive to your growth and advancement.

Ensuring that you are constantly surrounded by the right environment can easily be done by utilizing what I call the in-and-out method. This method can be used to help position you in an environment that will help your growth and trajectory. Simply put, if you are currently in a positive, high-vibrational, and supportive environment, it's best to stay in that environment because it has a high probability of setting you up for success. On the contrary, if your environment is negative, low-vibrational, and one that does not resonate with your energy or spirit, it's best to get out of it as soon as possible (you'll thank yourself in the future).

Distancing yourself from low-vibrational environments is important because they are extremely damaging to your physical, mental, spiritual, and emotional well-being. Low-vibrational environments also tremendously stifle your learning and growth by exacerbating the challenges associated with achieving your goals. If you want to remove yourself from this type of environmental trap, you must change your mentality and actions first. Since doing the same actions will only yield the same results, you must be mentally prepared and unafraid to go against the social norms and beliefs of the very low-vibrational environment that you wish to escape from. Once this is accomplished, your desired reality will follow.

On the other hand, if it seems like accomplishing your goals and getting to the next level in your life is still somehow evading you, despite already dwelling in a positive and supportive environment, then introspection and self-reflection could help you determine why your already positive environment and resources seem not to be enough for you. For this circumstance, it is worth knowing that a barrier of complacency and a lack of inspiration often exists. For example, the roots of a tree grown in a container eventually become root-bound over time as the tree grows and matures. When this happens, the roots run out of space and begin to wrap around each other as they try to escape their suppressing environment to find more space. For the tree to remain healthy, it must be repotted into a larger nutrient-dense pot (or, of course the earth) so that it has more room to grow. If you are indeed in a positive environment, but feel like you have reached a plateau, it may be because you have outgrown your pot (environment) and absorbed most of the nutrients (knowledge) that your surroundings have to offer, leaving you no room or opportunity to continue growing (root-bound). If this is the case, quickly get out of the environment that no longer serves you (albeit, once perfect for you) and place yourself into another high-vibrational and supportive space where you can continue to grow. Always remember that staying in an environment that you've outgrown will eventually become harmful to you.

Environment is your second gem! Use it as a reminder to make sure that you are always in a healthy environment so that you can continue to grow, thrive, and reach your goals.

NOTES

_____
_____
_____
_____
_____
_____
_____
_____
_____
_____
_____
_____
_____
_____
_____
_____
_____
_____
_____
_____
_____
_____
_____
_____
_____
_____

NOTES

CONFIDENCE

"Believe in yourself
like your life
depends on it,
because it does."

Confidence is another important tool that is beneficial for your growth and advancement. Being confident means being strong, bold, and certain of yourself and your abilities. With confidence, you embody and maintain a high-vibrational power that helps to shape your overall experiences and success. Without it, you are mentally confined to a lower version of yourself-which consequently restricts you from becoming your highest self and securing opportunities for elevation and achievement.

Accomplishing your goals and living a powerful, beautiful, and rewarding life is possible through confidence. Confidence gives you the braveness to run the race and the wings to fly across the finish line. Taking the time to learn how to cultivate the power of confidence elevates your thinking, boosts your power of magnetism, and teaches you how to trust and believe in yourself at a greater capacity. People who are highly confident in their abilities operate on a higher mental frequency and have a high level of self-efficacy. They maintain high vibrational thoughts, take time to build trust within themselves, have a tremendous amount of self-assurance, and have a deep desire to continuously learn and grow. Confident people also tend to be extremely successful because they constantly seek opportunities to push themselves into higher capacities while maintaining mental toughness, awareness, optimism, and clarity.

Confidence is exhibited in two different forms - internal and external. Your combined level of internal and external confidence determines your overall level of self-esteem and self-belief. Internal confidence is developed through a multitude of factors, including your choices, habits, natural gifts, competence, truthfulness, and awareness. This type of confidence is also directly attributed to your experiences in life and (most importantly) the amount of hunger you have to constantly push yourself to become better. Overall, internal confidence paves the way for external confidence and is reached once you have a high level of self-certainty and a deep understanding of the power of manifestation. External confidence is hugely influenced and amplified through various environmental factors and is the visible evidence of your mastery of internal confidence.

Developing confidence is one of the best things you can do to increase the possibility of attracting the life that you want. One of the biggest mistakes you could ever make is not being confident in yourself and choosing to live a life filled with fear, doubt, and regret. On the road to developing confidence, you must train your mind to withstand moments of difficulty and failure and to accept the challenges that will push you to become better. Fear and doubt should absolutely hold no place in your mind or heart. Instead, let the mistakes and missed opportunities of the fearsome be the guiding motivation for your confidence and success. Walk head held high confidently toward your dreams and believe that you will accomplish your goals in divine timing.

Confidence is your third gem! Learn to be confident in all you do - to be confident when you're right, to be confident when you're wrong, to be confident when you're weak, to be confident when you're strong. Be confident even if others doubt you or are intimidated by your power, energy, and purpose. Never diminish your light to make others feel better about themselves. Instead, shine as bright as you can while inspiring and demanding others around you to grow. Allow confidence to radiate through all your thoughts, actions, and endeavors. Build your level of confidence so great that others spiritually feel it as soon as you walk in a room. Build your confidence so high that you demand respect before you even utter a word. Allow confidence to consume your existence and ignore anything or anybody that tries to stand in the way of you living a confident life. Internalize this truth, combine it with your previous gems, and get to work - confidently.

NOTES

NOTES

VISION

"Those who have great sight see first with the mind's eye."

Visualization, as it relates to your purpose, is seeing not through the lens of your limited and often deceiving eyes, but through the power of your limitless mind. More specifically, visualization is you using your mind to clearly see a desired outcome before it exists or is visible to others. Visualization is one of the most powerful things that you can do while working towards your goals because it is extremely effective at helping you to remain focused and guiding you where you need and want to be. The clearer your vision is, and the more consistent you are at working towards it, the easier it is for you to accomplish your goals.

Setting goals is undoubtedly one of the best ways for you to plan for the future. However, the goals you set for yourself will amount to nothing unless you also have the vision to execute them. The first step to executing your goals is to visualize yourself accomplishing them within your mind. Visualization is so powerful (through intention, focus, and belief) that the universe begins working on bringing your vision into reality as soon as you clearly see it in your mind, begin putting in the work towards it, and believe in it wholeheartedly.

Since visualization is your present self mentally seeing and believing in a future reality for yourself, it is incredibly important for you to be cautious of what you visualize for yourself. The wrong vision can cause ruin and destruction in your life, while the right vision can steer you towards becoming a higher version of yourself. Becoming a higher version of yourself means learning how to trust yourself, your internal sight, and the process of manifestation more. If you lack trust in yourself, or vision for your life, you will always be consumed within the vision of someone else and never fully step into your purpose to build your own legacy.

What you consistently think of has the power to come true because your thoughts are energy and an extension of God (more on this in the next gem). If you can visualize it in your mind, then have faith that it can happen. Don't worry or concern yourself with how it will happen. Just keep working and believe that it is already done. Trust that visualization, if done with love for yourself and the world around you (with no malice or ill will towards anyone else), can raise your frequency and attract higher-vibrational people, places, and things to you that can assist you along your journey and development.

Understand that vision comes before success. Visualize yourself accomplishing your goals, move on them strategically, and execute them by any means (when vision, preparation, and strategy meet opportunity). Take the necessary steps to get to where you envision yourself, make the appropriate adjustments along the way to ascend to a higher version of yourself, and never veer the course of greatness no matter what.

Vision is your fourth gem! Visualize the life you want so that the universe and your subconscious mind work together to attract everything to you. Believe that so long as you can see it, it already is.

NOTES

NOTES

MASTER
YOUR MIND

"A person who masters their mind masters their actions. A person who masters their actions masters their life."

Your mind is the most beautiful and powerful tool in the world because it is a direct extension of the grand intelligence of God. Through the power of your mind, you can conceptualize, magnetize, and manifest anything that you desire using everlasting universal laws and principles. Having the ability to influence your external reality by the power and application of your own mind is not only an amazing gift from God, but also an incredible blessing that comes with immense responsibility. With such enormous responsibility, opportunity, and power, it is imperative that you completely understand how to control and master your mind.

Mastering your mind is one of the greatest feats that you can accomplish here in the physical realm because it is not only one of the hardest things to do, but also the ultimate key to unlocking your full potential. To manifest your greatest potential, or garner any sustainable form of success, you first need to adequately explore, understand, and master how you think and interpret information. More specifically, you need to fully understand the consequences of your thoughts and how they make you feel. Understanding the power of your thoughts is very important because you will eventually experience and ultimately become whatever it is that you continuously think about and give energy to. This means that if your thoughts are constantly positive and aligned with your life's purpose, then you will constantly experience a purposeful and high-vibrational reality. However, if your thoughts are consistently negative, and are in no way connected to your purpose, then you can unfortunately expect to consistently have low-vibrational experiences.

Without positive thinking, mastering your mind and becoming the best version of yourself is unattainable. Positive thinking is vital for the visualization and manifestation of your goals, and extremely necessary for great mental health. No one or nothing can hold you back if you are able to rise above any low-vibrational thoughts, experiences, or other forms of negativity. By remaining positive and eliminating negative thoughts from your mind, you allow yourself to remain mentally and spiritually balanced, which allows and prepares you to receive greater blessings. Always aim to maintain a positive mindset because doing so will significantly improve the quality of your life. It will keep your frequency and vibration high, heal you from past failures and traumas, and align you with the future that you seek and desire.

Since thoughts shape and influence who we are as individuals, and the way we see and interpret the world around us, it is also essential that we learn how to mind our minds at all times. "Minding your mind" is a component of mastering your mind where you make an intentional effort to guard your own thoughts (and energy) by training your mind what, when, and how to think. This form of self-control will make a huge difference in your outcomes and experiences in life because it works as a high-vibrational filtration system - wherein negative energy and unproductive thoughts get constantly eliminated by your own internal defense system. Always mind your mind and give your energy only to the things that serve you.

Mastering your mind will certainly catapult you to higher levels in your life (both internally and externally) by preparing you to think, approach, and handle situations properly. When you choose to master your mind, you choose to become a higher version of yourself and are more capable of reaching greatness. At this level of mental discipline and self-mastery, you can open any door that you want in life. Even better, at this level of mental self-protection, you will only attract the doors that vibrate in harmony with your purpose and spirit.

Mastering your mind is your fifth gem! Stay focused and seek mental stability and clarity. Don't fall for temptations or fall victim to negativity. Reaching your goals is just as much about the things that you don't do as it is about the things that you do. Accept the responsibility of your purpose and use your mind to masterfully take your vision from planning to execution. Always remember that to mind your mind is to mind your future, and to mind your future is to mind your legacy. Stay optimistic and calculated and approach your goals tactfully and intelligently. Envision where you want to be and trust that it will come to fruition. Believe that if you can see it in your mind, you can manifest it in the physical.

NOTES

NOTES

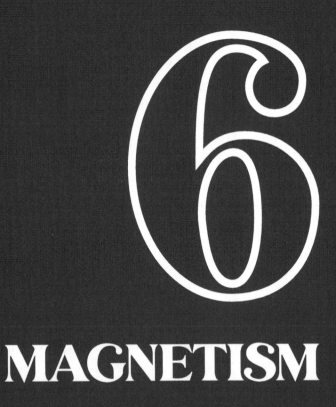

6

MAGNETISM

"You either attract
what you want or
what you don't want.
The choice is yours."

Most people understand that magnetism refers to attraction of some sort. However, most do not understand how to effectively use magnetism to accomplish their goals and attract success. Magnetism within this context is extremely powerful and involves using high-level thoughts, practices, methods, and principles to your advantage to help you attract what you desire. Once you fully understand magnetism, anything you desire is truly possible.

To understand magnetism more in this context, you need to fully understand the connection between magnetism and your mind. Your mind is one of the most powerful magnets in the universe and is indeed capable of manifesting what it thinks and visualizes. The process of magnetism is so powerful that it is done on both a conscious and subconscious level. Through its limitless power of conceptualization and magnetism, your mind is constantly attracting things to you - both what you do and don't want to experience. For this reason, it is very important to learn how to properly use your thoughts, principles, methods, and practices positively and in high-form so that you are mindful of what you are attracting at all times.

Since magnetism happens regardless, it's best to intentionally use its power to your advantage. When it comes to accomplishing your goals and obtaining success, high-level magnetism can be easily applied through the power of your mind. Again, if you think positively, then you will attract positivity. If you think negatively, then you will attract negative outcomes and experiences. If you think in terms of success, then you will attract success. It's really that simple. Think about what you want and allow your mind to magnetize it to you.

One practice that could be used daily to boost the power of your magnetism on a deeper and more powerful level is mindfulness. Mindfulness is the state of being intentionally present and aware of all your thoughts, communications, and activities. It is very important to always be mindful of what you are thinking and attracting. Being present in the moment (aware of yourself and circumstances) frees you from the shackles of distractions, comparison, judgment, and stubbornness and places you in a healthier mental state to make wiser decisions and garner a deeper understanding of yourself.

Another very useful practice that will help you to increase the power of your magnetism is speaking things into existence. Speaking things into existence and magnetism go hand-in-hand. Successful people believe in the power of the tongue and tend to speak their desired accomplishments and future into existence. Repeating this practice will tremendously boost your faith and amplify your power of both magnetism and manifestation. By doing so, you will also realize that the more you speak things into existence, the more likely and faster things will manifest for you (more in-depth discussion on this later in the book).

Magnetism is your sixth gem! Whatever your current level in life is, who you interact with, and even how you found out about this book all stem from the same place - your mind and attraction. Whether consciously or subconsciously, you directly attract and are responsible for your experiences in life. This is why it is incredibly important to focus on the things that you want to attract, versus fixating on the things that you don't. Learn to become comfortable with being fully consumed with your vision and with the process of manifesting it. Act, talk, think, dress, and walk like what you want to attract because your mind is always working to magnetize the reality that you focus on and desire. Become one with your vision and magnetize what you want while repelling what you don't. Speak into existence that you will accomplish your goals and that success is yours in abundance. Think it and become it. Claim it and proclaim it. Believe it and see it.

NOTES

NOTES

PURPOSE

"Your purpose is bigger than you."

Finding your purpose in life is one of the most important things you could ever do. Purpose gives you meaning, happiness, success, and liberation and empowers you with love, harmony, balance, and high-vibrational experiences. Without purpose, your life will be aimless and stricken with enormous ignorance, disappointment, and regret. You will also unfortunately experience the anguish and misfortune of constantly being moved around chaotically by the currents of life.

The reason countless people are miserable and unable to live a fulfilling life is because they have no clue what their purpose is or what they're called to do. Even sadder, there are people who have never given it any thought. As a result, these people dwell in a lower vibrational plane full of anger, unfulfillment, and unhappiness. Finding out your purpose will help you to avoid this unnecessary hurt and harm. If you don't want to be like the countless people who don't know who they truly are, or who they're meant to be because they haven't pondered the thought or spiritually searched for the answer, I urge you to deeply question your life's true meaning and calling and find the answer.

Simply put, your purpose is your guiding light to be who you are uniquely called to be and do what you were called to do. It gives you direction in life, a blueprint to vocation, a reason to wake up in the morning, and a way to make a difference in the lives of others. The path to finding your divine purpose is a personal and introspective quest that involves moving with humility so that the answer can be revealed to you. Although some believe that the road to figuring out your purpose is a long and difficult process, I couldn't disagree more. An easy way to find and understand your purpose (at least the root of it) is to first figure out what your God given gift is. This gift will be obvious to you because it will be the thing that you love to do, have intuitive knowledge and skill in (it just makes sense to you and feels right), and what people thank you for. An aspect of your purpose then is to share whatever that gift is with the rest of the world.

Although every person is born with a unique purpose and set of gifts to influence the world, few people understand and accept their individual path and have the discipline to operate solely in it. This happens for a variety of reasons, usually from a lack of humility, judgement, comparison, or ignorance. One thing that is certain is that living outside of your purpose is unwise because it leads you down a path of unnecessary hardship. This is because choosing not to live in your purpose is akin to swimming upstream a strong river current. Understand that your purpose will never forsake you and will always lead you to an abundance of happiness, blessings, opportunities, and prosperity. No matter what it is, or how small or simple you may think your gift may be, trust in it and yourself. If that isn't enough, trust that there is a reason why God gave you the gift.

Purpose is your seventh gem! Finding your purpose is your sole obligation - and a massive obligation it is. Your purpose is the quintessential foundation of your life. Once you discover what your true purpose in life is, you should immediately begin centering as much of your life around it as possible. Don't miss or dismiss your calling. Never hide, neglect, or ignore your purpose because you think that your gift won't be accepted by others or provide you with the life you want. Always remember that ignoring your purpose is destructive. Become who you are meant to be and do what you are called to do. Stay in your lane and avoid the temptation to compare yourself with others. Treat your purpose with immense respect and use it to escape the illusion of limitations. Choose to operate in your purpose because it will place you in rooms you can't fathom or never thought possible. Remove any person, place, or thing from your life that is not aligned with your purpose, no matter how difficult it may be or how attached you are to it. Since your purpose defines your life, the decisions you make regarding protecting it are crucial. Be assertive in seeking your purpose, aggressive in protecting it, and bold in living it.

NOTES

NOTES

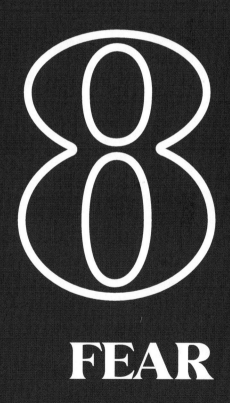

FEAR

"It's ok to be
afraid sometimes.
However, it's never ok
to let fear hold you back
from your dreams."

Too many people fail to accomplish their goals because they are stuck in a low-vibrational mental barrier of fear. Fear is often what separates those who go for their dreams from those who don't. Yes, fear is a normal human emotion that everyone experiences at one point or another. However, strong and successful people find the courage to face their fears and don't allow their fears to hold them back. They understand that fear is not of God and that you must have a strong and fearless mentality to succeed. At the very least, when it comes to fear, have the courage to still go for your dreams even if you are afraid.

Fear is like an infection. If left untreated, it will eventually cause more and more harm. This is why it is important to always confront and control your fears. Living in fear is incredibly foolish because it prevents you from living a high-vibrational life. Succumbing to fear invites low-vibrational frequencies into your life such as regret, anger, depression, and envy. The longer you dwell in this low-vibrational state, the more you doubt yourself and become harmed by those powerful types of hindering energies. Do not hold yourself back simply because you're afraid of the unknown. Think positively and become fearless.

Whenever fear presents itself in any form, remember that you have the power to use it to your advantage. Facing your fears is advantageous because it turns your weaknesses into strengths, which undoubtedly leads to increased motivation, growth, and elevation in your life. Whenever you are fearful, remind yourself that the feeling is only temporary (which is empowering). Also, remain steadfast in your faith that you can accomplish anything that you desire. If you're afraid of failing, remember that failure is only a precursor to success. If you're afraid of starting, remember that you can't win a race unless you begin moving. If you're afraid of making mistakes, remember that you won't grow without them. If you're afraid that you don't have the knowledge, skills, resources, time, or support to accomplish your dreams, remember that the universe will always provide everything you need once you take a leap of faith.

Conquering your fears is your eighth gem! Yes, fear is real and can be difficult to overcome, but what's scarier than going through life never having the courage to bet on yourself and go after your dreams?

NOTES

NOTES

CIRCUMSTANCE

"An unfortunate
circumstance
doesn't define you.
The will and mindset
to change it does."

It takes a mature and optimistic mind to understand that any unfortunate circumstance can change for the better at any given moment in time. Living a happy life is predicated on this truth. It takes an even more mature mind to truly understand how that change is initiated. The reality and circumstances we experience are the external reflections of our internal compositions. In other words, the universe is constantly projecting our inner thoughts, understandings, and beliefs. From this, it then becomes clear that every person has the innate ability to change their circumstance through the will and application of their own mind. Ultimately, the understanding and application of this truth is the difference between experiencing a temporary setback or permanent failure.

As previously mentioned, people attract the circumstances they experience, whether consciously or subconsciously (magnetism). As spiritual beings on this human journey, we experience this world temporarily and understand the necessity and eventuality of change. However, while your experiences and circumstances are guaranteed to constantly change, you do have the power to change them to whatever you want. This means that your circumstance can either become the motivation you need to reach and keep success, or it can become the excuse you'll sadly use as to why you never accomplished your goals. Choose wisely.

If you want to change your circumstance for the better, first view it through the lens of positivity (as hard as it may seem). It's also important to understand the difference between who you are and the situation that you are experiencing. Never fall into a low-vibrational mindset or pattern of entertaining negativity, especially regarding yourself. Remind yourself that you are blessed and that you have the power to change your circumstances at any moment. Remember that things could always be worse, that it's normal to experience unfavorable circumstances, and that others have gone through (or are currently experiencing) the same thing or something similar.

Changing your undesired circumstance is both humbling and rewarding because it shows you who you truly are and how you handle adversity. Are you the type to win or whine? Will you focus or fold? Will you give it your all or give it all up? If you let it, the process and pressure of changing your circumstance for the better will build your character, teach you patience, strengthen your faith, and prepare you to face and overcome any form of difficulty or challenge.

Handling undesired circumstances is your ninth gem! Remember that being unsatisfied breeds hunger and that hunger breeds a very powerful and focused individual. Weather the storm and never let your circumstance or difficulties determine who you are or how you feel about yourself. Know that you absolutely have the power to change both your circumstances and the world. Just make sure that you are changing them for the better.

NOTES

NOTES

PART I END

Part I provides you with the necessary insight and wisdom to form a powerful foundation (the roots) for your tree of success. Before any external change can happen in your life, you must first change your thoughts, patterns, vision, beliefs, attitudes, and habits to be more aligned with your higher self and God. The high-vibrational gems contained within Part I are the keys to growth, manifestation, magnetism, and success because they provide the foundation for other branches of success to form, show you how to transform your mind, and teach you how to transcend your circumstances.

Change your mentality for the better and think carefully, critically, and responsibly. Believe in yourself always, and in all ways. Never let your unwanted circumstances deflate your confidence or have power over you or your life. Never give in to fear. As sure as old habits die hard, so too will your dreams if you don't protect them or take the necessary steps to accomplish them. Work hard, live in your purpose, and watch how your life changes for the better with a solid foundation.

PART II

WORKING TOWARDS
MANIFESTATION & SUCCESS
(THE TRUNK)

"WITHOUT FOCUS, THERE IS NO PROGRESS. WITHOUT
PROGRESS, THERE IS NO SUCCESS."

PATIENCE

"When you are patient,
you are humble.
When you are humble,
you are wise."

One of the greatest lessons in life is learning to be patient. Patience is beautiful and rewarding. As the well-known saying goes, "good things come to those who wait." Waiting on things to happen for you in your own divine timing is the purest form of patience, trust, and understanding. By waiting, it shows that you don't force things to happen, but rather that you wisely submit to God's plan and timing over your life.

Learning to be patient equips you with a form of self-mastery and empowers you with a higher form of wisdom and discipline that you can use to your advantage. In its essence, patience is a form of trust, humility, and stillness. Since patience is hard to acquire and master, having it shows that your decisions aren't solely predicated on temporary gratification. Instead, patience shows that you are focused on honestly and properly laying the foundation for your success, without concern of when it will happen. In fact, true patience demands that you remove any preconceived expectation of how things should happen or go for you. At this level of humility and maturity, you understand the importance of relinquishing your illusion of control and begin to seek knowledge from sources greater than your own limited understanding.

One reason people give up on their dreams is simply because they are impatient. Since most people fear the unknown, and not having control, they often lack the mental preparation and emotional stability to put in continuous work on their goals without knowing exactly when it will pay off. Whether it takes you one day to accomplish your goals, or twenty years, keep going until you reach the finish line. While there are ways to expedite and increase your probability of reaching success, the exact timing of its manifestation remains out of your control. Understanding and accepting this reality is yet another thing that separates those who give up on their dreams from those who grind until they reach success, no matter how long it takes.

Patience is your tenth gem! When you exercise patience, you are consciously choosing to be still and trust in your own timing. If you have been working extremely hard on your goals so that you can one day live the life you desire, keep going strong. Remember that accomplishing your goals will happen if and only if you believe that it will happen, exercise patience, and constantly put in the work. If you are experiencing doubt because you haven't reaped the benefits of your hard work yet, then remind yourself that patience is key. Trust that God will never forsake you and that things will happen for you in divine timing. Keep your faith and motivation, continue to put in the work, and watch how your blessings appear before your eyes. It's truly not a matter of if it will happen, only when.

NOTES

NOTES

11

PRESSURE

"Handle the pressure in your life before it handles you."

Along your journey to success, you can expect at some point to encounter some form of pressure. Pressure is a necessary component to reaching success. You can either allow pressure to make you better. Or you can let it negatively affect you and break your spirit. Pressure comes in both positive and negative forms. Positive pressure pushes you to grow and evolve, especially in your purpose. Negative pressure, on the other hand, is often external to your purpose and is a form of unnecessary suffering that disrupts and siphons your energy. Always aim to eliminate all negative pressure from your life (although understandably, there are times when this is not possible).

Pressure is all about how you handle it. For many, pressure brings out the best in them. One of the easiest ways to deal with pressure is to recall a previous experience when you overcame pressure (we all have experienced this at one point or another) by having a fighting spirit. As difficult as that time may have been, taking the time to remember how you persevered through that situation, and how you grew and became stronger through the process, will give you renewed strength to deal with your current pressure and confidence that all will work out in your favor. That's the true beauty of pressure; it makes you stronger if you let it.

No matter how difficult it is, never run from the pressure of your purpose. This is extremely important because we tend to run from the very thing(s) that could help us grow the most. Running from the pressure of your purpose will only inhibit your growth (the negative psychological effect you would endure from repeating cowardice actions) and set you back. Instead of running or hiding, meet the pressure of your purpose head held high and ten toes down. Always remain open to learning. Again, if you let it, pressure will breed a warrior spirit within you. Akin to weight-lifting, the more weight that you are subjected to, the stronger you become. Being subjected to pressure is also a great way to identify your areas of weakness so that you can improve upon them. Admittedly, the key is finding the right balance as being placed under too much pressure is dangerous. However, as you begin to get used to the weight (pressure) of your purpose and develop more strength and endurance from working and never quitting, you will gradually see yourself become stronger.

Since pressure is one of the greatest motivators for success, you must also apply pressure on yourself (another form of positive pressure) if you truly want to grow, evolve, and transform your life. This means continuously holding yourself accountable, lighting a fire under yourself to accomplish your goals, and eliminating all excuses. Having this mentality demands a higher version of yourself (a version that fiercely and unapologetically executes goals by any means). Applying positive pressure on yourself significantly levels you up because it teaches you trust, self-discipline, and accountability. It also eliminates any reliance or expectations you have of others. Instead, operating at this frequency allows you to trust in yourself and God more. Once you adopt this mentality, and apply it to all you do, you become a walking form of positive pressure to yourself and everyone around you.

Pressure is your eleventh gem! If you haven't reached where you want to be in life yet, pressure may be what you need to move forward. Enough pressure can produce a positive change in your mindset and actions. Always hold yourself to the highest level of accountability and never let pressure hold you back from greatness.

NOTES

NOTES

12

CONSISTENCY

"A book is written one word at a time."

Imagine a person so focused on their purpose that most of their time and energy consistently revolves around accomplishing their goals. A person who, despite numerous moments of failure, still has a ferocious drive to succeed. A person who doesn't believe in making excuses and who refuses to let anyone outwork them. A person who has no doubt in their mind that they will succeed because they work hard every day to turn their dreams into reality. Now, be honest whether the person that was just described sounds like you. If it doesn't, then you aren't working nearly as hard or consistently as you think you are or should be. Imagine how your life would be and what you would accomplish if you turned into that person.

Consistency paves the way for success. Every person has a choice to either be consistent in their efforts, or inconsistent. This is extremely important because the level of success you will most likely achieve depends on your level of commitment and consistency. Simply put, those who are consistent, consistently succeed; and those who are consistently inconsistent succeed only at wasting time and energy. Successful people work until they reach their goals (no matter how long they take), never give in to failure, and remain consistent in their pursuit of individual greatness. They also deeply understand the process and power of laying one brick at a time (through patience and consistency, eventually something great can be built).

Work ethic and consistency go hand-in-hand. Both are a huge reflection of your level of discipline and are reliable indicators of success. Once you develop the proper mindset, work ethic, and consistency, your results will only increase (at this point, it then only becomes a game of patience). Being consistent and having a great work ethic will always provide opportunities for more learning, growth, and experience; all of which are necessary for reaching success.

Consistency requires a very strong and serious mindset. This is because success requires you to remain consistent when things are going well, and also when they aren't. When things aren't going the best, remember that it's when you're the closest to reaching your goals that things tend to go the most wrong or become the most chaotic. These moments are a test of not only your character, but also of your heart, mind, will, discipline, and focus. Ultimately, your work ethic and consistency during these moments will determine your future circumstances and outcomes. In all that you do, and in all that you encounter, understand that it's vital for you to remain diligent and consistent in your efforts towards success. Again, although it may seem at times as if your hard work isn't paying off, keep going. Even if things are manifesting slower than you may have wanted or envisioned, reframe your mind to look at it as though they are manifesting quicker than you realize.

If you want to be great, work on yourself and build your own path. The road to greatness is the road less traveled because most are unwilling to be consistent and make the sacrifices to become great (time, money, energy, sleep, relationships, etc.). Most people are also very uncomfortable being uncomfortable and can't fathom experiencing a period of being "without" or going through immense change. Knowing that only a few people are truly willing to sacrifice their temporary comforts (and remain consistent in doing so) should deeply inspire and motivate you to not let fear or change deter you from your dreams.

Consistency is your twelfth gem! If you work hard and remain consistent on your goals, you immediately set yourself apart from most people in the world. No matter how many doors close, stay confident, remain consistent, and keep working. The doors that close only make sure that the right ones open for you in the future. Be consistent in building your path to success. Stay true to your dreams, focused throughout the process, and consistent in your work, time, and effort. Use the gem of consistency to quit quitting on yourself. Use it to break the cycle of not breaking the cycle. Use it to become free and to change your life for the better.

NOTES

NOTES

13

DISCIPLINE

"Discipline is the
father of consistency
and the blueprint
of success."

For most people, achieving success will not be a quick, easy, and effortless process; especially for those who lack vision, drive, and determination. Instead, success for most will be the result of hard work, consistency, and discipline. Of all the necessary components that lead to success and manifestation, discipline ranks very high on the list of importance and should be practiced and mastered by all.

Discipline is one of the greatest qualities that you can have because it is a gateway to increased understanding, mastery, skill, focus, and opportunity. True discipline is developed through self-mastery and when your thoughts and actions become deeply motivated and influenced by your obsession to succeed. Once your desire to succeed becomes greater than your fear of failure, discipline emerges to steer you towards an abundance of growth, stability, and opportunity and to keep you anchored to your purpose.

Discipline is the avenue to increased accomplishment and manifestation. People who are extremely disciplined become masters of manifesting their visions because they understand the laws of the universe. More specifically, they understand the importance of being focused and maintaining a superior work ethic. A person of great discipline will easily move mountains through means of their own will, focus, and self-mastery; while a person who lacks discipline will only move further away from their true self and calling. All highly productive and successful people have discipline. To have discipline is to know and understand God and to have power and control of yourself. For this reason, seeking, developing, and exercising discipline is a necessity if you plan to become a better version of yourself.

Putting in the work every day to make sure that you are constantly growing and continuously moving closer to accomplishing your goals is a form of discipline. Discipline is locking in on your goals, getting things done whether you feel like it or not, and staying focused until you see results (and even beyond). Although having discipline is a beautiful thing, there is nothing pretty or easy about developing and practicing it because it requires mental toughness, commitment, and sacrifice. If you want to increase the probability of accomplishing your goals, disciplining your thoughts and actions (mentality) must become a welcomed habit.

Discipline is your thirteenth gem! There is no question that discipline leads to increased accomplishment and fruitfulness. Being disciplined will always be necessary for success and bring out the best version of yourself. Discipline your mind first, then watch your actions and success follow. Remember that the greater the discipline a person has, the greater their advantage in life. Allow discipline to guide you towards increased order and manifestation. Understand that improvement does not exist without consistent effort, and consistent effort not without discipline. Be disciplined until greatness consumes all areas of your life, and even then, maintain your discipline, focus, and power and keep going.

NOTES

NOTES

14

BET ON
YOURSELF

"The greatest risk
you can take
is not taking
a risk at all."

Life is a beautiful symphony of choices. Through all your experiences and choices in life, betting on yourself is one of the greatest things that you can choose to do. No matter who you are, betting on yourself is an absolute must. When you bet on yourself, you exhibit the ultimate faith in yourself and your dreams. Betting on yourself should never be a second option, but rather the only option. Never be afraid to trust in yourself, take risks, and go for what you want. No matter the circumstance, or how many failures you experience, betting on yourself is always the right thing to do.

If you don't believe in yourself, or never take the steps to go for your dreams, then how can you expect others to? You can't and they won't. Always have faith in yourself and your vision and work consistently to make it a reality. After all, your goals aren't going to accomplish themselves. Those who exhibit faith are blessed beyond measure. This is because anything is possible if you have faith that all things are possible. Any successful person will tell you that they reached their goals because they first thought that it was possible. They also will tell you that manifesting your dreams requires confidence in your abilities and faith that everything will work in your favor. If you consistently doubt yourself and your abilities, then you can be sure that the same low vibrational energy will return to you in the future and become a deterrent towards your progress.

Faith will comfort you in times of defeat, shield you in times of weakness, save you in times of doubt, and guide you when you're lost. Faith keeps you centered, provides armor and reassurance, and stokes the fire you have to reach your goals and success. It also allows you to connect to your higher self and keeps you connected to your purpose. When you are lost for answers, or backed into a corner, or when opportunity presents itself for you to carve your own lane, remember to have faith and to always bet on yourself.

Betting on yourself is your fourteenth gem! When you choose to bet on yourself, you choose to have faith. When you choose to have faith, you choose yourself, your purpose, and God. Operating in your own lane and taking risks is the only way to keep you from living your life centered around someone else's purpose (again, those who have denied their purpose or allowed it to be sequestered by others are miserable). Remember that everything is cause and effect (more on this in gem 17), and that your faith, opportunities, perception, and work ethic dictate the quality of life that you will have. Also, remember that you are the only person who truly knows the intricacies of your purpose and dreams. Have faith in your unique calling, sow into your dreams by investing in yourself, never fear walking your path alone, and fully trust that the universe has your back and that it will send you the resources you need to assist you on your journey. Have faith that God is ordering your footsteps, even when you can't see the path yourself. Have faith that it will all work out in your favor. Have the courage to bet on yourself, always and in all ways.

NOTES

NOTES

15

TRUST THE
PROCESS

"Everything is in
perfect timing."

Doubt is another main reason why people remain stagnant and never accomplish their goals. Although everyone experiences doubt at some point in their life, the key to being successful is to never let doubt control you. Being doubtful (particularly regarding your goals) is a huge waste of time, energy, and thought because it is immensely detrimental to your confidence, growth, and overall advancement. More specifically, doubting whether your hard work and sacrifices will lead to positive and successful outcomes implies not only that you don't fully trust in yourself or your abilities, but more importantly that you don't fully trust God. The more you doubt yourself and God (and never doubt God), the less likely it will be for you to manifest the life that you want.

If you truly desire to accomplish all your goals and excel in life, you must learn to doubt your doubts and to trust the process. Trusting the process means believing that the universe is always working for (and through) you, understanding that every step of your journey has value and purpose, and humbly accepting that you are currently where you need to be in life, whatever level or location that may be. Letting go of doubt and completely trusting the process allows you to operate at a high-vibrational state of calm and trust, which in turn leads to increased productivity with your visions and implementations in life. Additionally, believing that the universe is working in your divine favor also leads to increased harmony, wisdom, connection, perspective, optimism, and understanding of the everlasting power and brilliance of God.

As one could assume, trusting the process is easier said than done. To become comfortable trusting the process, you must first understand and accept that you aren't in control of anything other than your own actions. Abiding by this simple yet powerful truth helps you to put things into greater perspective and approach situations more wisely. Secondly, to both embody and reflect the notion of what trusting the process truly means, you also must master how to separate yourself from your ego (more about ego in Part III) and let go of your desire to control every aspect of your life. Once you deeply understand both of these powerful components of trusting the process, you will quickly become better positioned to continuously attract greater wisdom, abundance, blessings, and prosperity.

During your journey to enlightenment and success, learning to trust the process is undoubtedly one of the biggest tests of your faith. Instead of leaning on your own understanding, or (and especially) letting your ego unwisely influence your decisions, allow yourself to completely trust in the wisdom of God and to be guided by His will and timing for your life. When you are fearless, confident, and obedient, life will happen for you (favor) instead of to you. More specifically, when you let go of control, you accept the good and the bad, the highs and the lows, and the perfect timing of them all, which is a very beautiful, spiritual, and liberating space to be in. Remember that trusting the process is rooted in faith and that your life is working in divine order. Keep your vibration high, exercise faith and wisdom in all your endeavors, appreciate every precious moment of your life, and always remain humble. Most importantly, remember that you are fully capable of anything you desire because you are, and will always be, an extension of the Most High.

Trusting the process is your fifteenth gem! Find comfort in the unknown and know that the power of the universe is behind you in all your righteous pursuits. Trust in something greater than yourself and believe with every ounce of your existence that your time is coming. Just as "faith of a mustard seed can move mountains," the opposite is also true in that even the smallest amount of doubt can hinder your progress and create unnecessary difficulties and delays for your success. Maintain your faith and allow it to be your strength and refuge during times of uncertainty. Allow your spirit to be your intelligent compass to manifestation and greatness. Remember that being doubtful is not only unproductive and highly pessimistic, but also a gateway to becoming addicted to excuses and complacency. Look within, tap into your higher consciousness, and be courageous in all your pursuits. Skip the doubt, do the work, trust the process, and watch the rest fall perfectly in place for you.

NOTES

NOTES

16
SILENCE

"Silence can
oftentimes speak
the loudest."

During your path to greatness, and as things begin to manifest for you, you will inevitably be faced with a plethora of challenges and distractions. Although being free of all distractions is ideal, it's important to learn how to avoid and remove them from your life when they do indeed present themselves. The best way to drown out the noise of distraction is silence. Silence is oftentimes the only thing that you need. Those who are successful understand the importance of silence and aren't afraid to use its power to assist them in their journey.

There are different forms, uses, and benefits of silence that you should be aware of. The first being the positive effect that it can have on your level of focus. It is often when we are alone and intentionally avoid distractions that we produce our best work. Taking a break from technology, work, or the company of others is extremely important because it keeps you balanced, reconnects you with yourself and with God, and can accelerate your growth. Being absent, or in silence, relieves you of constant stimuli, which can decrease your stress level and lead to better focus. Whenever you need to increase your productivity level, try seeking the comfort of silence.

Another benefit of silence is healing. The healing effects of silence are truly marvelous. The right amount of silence will heal your mind, body, and soul. No matter how extraverted you are, everyone needs time to themselves to recharge. As demanding as life can be, you must be diligent in your efforts to recharge. Interacting with others can drain your energy, even if only on a minuscule level. You are no good to others (or yourself) and will never accomplish your goals if you are constantly burned out. The key is having proper balance. Understand that it's more than ok to take time to yourself for mental health, focus, and creativity. Whenever you experience symptoms of being drained, overworked, or overwhelmed, it's a good idea to retreat into silence for yourself.

As sure as distractions are to come, again so to are moments of uncertainty at some point during your journey. When things are cloudy, confusing, or chaotic, the noise of your life and immediate environment have unfortunately drowned out your universal calm and balance. During these times, the purity of silence will quiet the world around you, show you the way, and guide you to the answers you seek. Being silent, still, and in the comfort of only yourself allows you to free your mind to hear the internal and divine direction of your purpose.

Another powerful aspect of silence that will always prove to be extremely useful during your path to greatness is learning to mind your tongue. Sometimes, the things you don't say (being silent) speak the loudest because there is great power in restraint. In situations where you could say something negative, don't. In times when you don't know the answer, don't pretend to. Wisdom is knowing when and when not to speak. Treat your words like they hold extreme weight and value. Choose your words as if they're limited only to the aspects of love, life, light, knowledge, and positivity.

Learning how to "move in silence" is another powerful aspect of silence. Moving in silence protects your peace and privacy. When you move in silence, you choose to demonstrate restraint, humility, and maturity by keeping yourself free from the motives, influence, and opinions of others. This is especially important when your dreams and ideas are still under construction. Remember that you work entirely too hard to be destroyed by loose lips (oversharing through lack of discernment). Not everything about yourself or your plans should be shared with others. Never boast or brag and always treat others with respect. More importantly, respect yourself and your purpose by doing your best to protect it.

Silence is your sixteenth gem! Silence helps you to calibrate and reset your focus towards your purpose and goals. In silence, you are able to recharge and grow by absorbing the power of peace and tranquility. Minimal interactions and distractions, coupled with maximum calmness, will always accelerate your recharge. Understand that silence is full of infinite wisdom and answers and that it will often speak loudly to you. Learn to listen to it keenly with an open mind. Remember that those who find silence, find stillness, and those who are still, find God. Work hard, keep your plans to yourself, and remember that silent moves produce loud results.

NOTES

NOTES

17

THE HIGHER
POWER

"All things are contained
within the mind of
the Most High."

Whether you know it or not, there exists a higher power within you that is infinitely great. The source of this power is "The Source" of all - God. No matter which name you use (God, The Source, The Creator, The Most High, The Higher Power, etc.), God in His brilliance and authority, is omnipotent, omniscient, omnipresent, and infinitely great. It is impossible to escape the presence of God because everything is held within His great and infinite mind. Believing in The Higher Power is supremely important to your purpose. Once you begin seeking a deeper connection to The Higher Power and understanding the principles that govern your overall existence and purpose, everything you desire will be fully in reach and manifest as they should through divine order and delivery.

Everything has always (and will continue to be) involved, revolved, and evolved around energy. God, in His eternal oneness, is the source of the energy we draw upon. God's energy is sacred and pure and is infinitely and supremely abundant in frequency and vibration. Since we are infinitely contained within the mind of God, we then are able to control the level of frequency we chose to operate in. As there are infinite levels of high vibrational planes of existence, there too are infinite levels of lower vibrational planes. Understanding this concept is crucial along your path to make sure that you are always vibrating in a high vibrational state, rather than a low one. Higher levels of frequency allow your mind to magnetize and manifest your thoughts in a purer and quicker form, while lower frequencies and planes of existence produce the opposite. With this, it's important to understand that reaching new levels of success will always require you to vibrate and function at a higher level than the one you are currently operating on.

To seek a deeper understanding of God is to seek a deeper understanding of yourself. We as humans are the projections of the eternal oneness, made in the image of an ethereal and universal existence. Our minds are only able to conceptualize, understand, and visualize this because of the infinite wisdom of God. More specifically, you are only able to magnetize your desires because you are connected to, and an extension of, the mind and power of God. Understanding this truth allows you to be able to live the life that you want and deserve. Trust in God because He will never forsake you. Ask Him the desires of your heart and behold the power of manifestation over your life.

One universal law that we are constantly subjected to, and that governs our existence, is the concept of cause and effect. To understand cause and effect is to understand the nature of God and the universe. This understanding significantly increases your productivity and ultimately determines your success. Simply put, cause and effect means that every action has a consequence. From this, it only makes sense to make sure that your actions are always rooted in love, light, and positivity. For example, if you are diligent in working hard on your purpose (cause), then by the supreme direction and intelligence of God, the universe is obliged to produce an effect for you related to this action (in this case, a positive effect). Since God will never fail you, the least that you can do is your part in working on the purpose that He bestowed upon you. All you have to do is start (faith of a mustard seed). Once you begin to work on your goals and within your purpose (faith without work is dead), He will position things in your favor.

Seeking The Higher Power is your seventeenth gem! Remain humble and remember that although you were made in the image of God, you will never be able to rise above Him. No matter who you are, what you have done, there is always more knowledge and wisdom to acquire. Give thanks for life and seek to understand the natural rhythm of your existence. Be patient, bide your time, and in a hurry for nothing. Trust in yourself and seek to understand God more so that you can acquire more knowledge, wisdom, and blessings.

NOTES

NOTES

18

REMEMBER
YOUR WHY

"**Your why is your** inspiration
to keep going."

No matter what level of success you obtain, knowing what's important to you and remembering what motivates you to keep going is extremely crucial. As you begin to set different things in motion, and as things begin to manifest, you must "remember your why." Your why is the meaning and purpose behind your actions. It is the reason you are willing to work towards a goal or task and is equally as important as your actions themselves. Without a why, you'll never truly have the drive to accomplish anything because there would be nothing intrinsically motivating you to do so. When you discover your why, you discover yourself.

Remembering your why will give you the strength to make it through any challenge or difficulty thrown your way. Whenever your faith is tested, remind yourself of the calling over your life and listen keenly to your inner voice. When you focus on what inspires you to work hard and keep going, you become an unstoppable juggernaut headed towards success. Your why will always be a source of strength and protection over your life because it is far greater than any obstacle standing in your path. As a rule, always to the best of your ability avoid pursuing things that won't bring you happiness or that aren't aligned with your why and purpose.

Remembering your why helps you stay true to yourself, keeps you real, and puts your intentions into perspective. This is especially useful when the things that you are working towards begin to manifest. As success begins to come, it becomes easy to lose focus and to get pulled away from your purpose. To avoid becoming lost and distracted by the flashing lights of success, never forget that your why should always be connected to the moves you make and energy you put out into the world (which is your anchor).

Remembering your why is your eighteenth gem! No matter how high you climb, remembering the true purpose of your journey and why you began to embark on it, will forever keep you humble and give you the strength to press forward. Your why is your motivation during times of adversity and strength during moments of uncertainty. It's what keeps you centered, balanced, and humble, and what helps you to never give up on your dreams. Your why defines who you are, and who (in greater depth) you are meant to be. When you remember your why, you forget anything else that is not aligned with your purpose. More importantly, when you remember your why, you never forget your way.

NOTES

NOTES

PART II END

The gems in Part II of this book were strategically selected to give you the wisdom and insight that you need in your transition from foundational work (Part I) to manifestation. The trunk, or the middle of your journey, is the period of laying the groundwork for your tree of success. The work that you put into manifesting your goals will ultimately make or break the sustainability of your progress and success. By applying the gems outlined in Part II, you will continue to build on your foundation and take successful steps forward.

Part II also teaches you that during your journey to self-improvement and success, it is of the utmost importance that you remain focused and humble once you begin to see progress and success. It's also very important to note that this is the absolute worst time to take your foot off the gas. Instead, the best thing to do once you see progress is to push even harder. By doing so, you continue to show God that you are ready and able to receive more divine blessings and wisdom, and that you are truly on a path to greatness.

Part II further teaches you how to manifest the desires of your heart and mind while giving you the wisdom to sustain them. Be diligent in understanding the gems outlined in both Parts I and II so that your life will continue to be filled with an abundance of blessings. Once your foundation is set, and your groundwork is laid, you automatically set yourself apart from others by ascending to a higher level of work, confidence, trust, understanding, and spirituality.

Give thanks for life and continue your quest to accomplish all your goals. Strong roots combined with a mighty trunk create the beautiful possibility of a bountiful and Godly crown.

Keep working, and trust that every day you are getting closer to your dreams!

PART III

REACHING & KEEPING SUCCESS (THE CROWN)

"THE KEY TO CONTINUED SUCCESS
IS TO STAY HUNGRY FOR MORE."

KEEP
WORKING

"When you are walking
in your purpose,
no distance is too great.
No road is too far."

Nothing in this universe is allowed to stand still. Everything is subjected to constant evolution and ascension upward. You too are of course also bound by this truth and obligation. No matter who you are, what you have, or what you have done, there are always more levels to climb and more knowledge and wisdom to obtain. Every day is an opportunity to learn and grow and should be met eagerly with a thirst to succeed. If you are not intentionally aiming to learn, grow, and evolve daily, you will never fully live in your purpose or up to your potential.

Knowledge will extend, enhance, and sustain your life and state of being. Those who are high-vibrational have higher-vibrational mindsets and never stop learning or trying to accomplish more. They wholeheartedly fear and rebuke complacency because they know that complacency suppresses creativity, passion, and work ethic. Under no circumstance should you ever become complacent. Complacency is dangerous and highly counterproductive. Never allow yourself to become stagnant or comfortable to the point that you stop making efforts towards growth and advancement. Always strive to reach higher levels of knowledge and success.

The aspiration to succeed and become better must exist if you want to accomplish your goals. Keep in mind that there will always be more to learn and improve on, even if you have risen to the top of your respective field. Remain mindful that there is always someone waiting to take your place. True innovators are never complacent and are always working on their next idea. Find the inspiration to keep going so that you can continue to innovate, learn, grow, and push the envelope further.

Keep working is your nineteenth gem! Never take your purpose for granted or underestimate your power. Believe that you are a catalyst of change and a beacon of light that must always keep ascending higher. Always live and work as if you are here to be a powerful change agent in our world by blessing others with your divine purpose. Always keep working for yours.

NOTES

NOTES

20

FIND YOUR
CALM

"The quality of your life
depends on your
mastery of balance."

Fully committing yourself to working towards your goals is by far one of the hardest things you can do in life because of the countless time, effort, and sacrifices required to do so. Pressure, as previously mentioned in Part II, is one reason why countless people give up on their dreams, and why only a few truly commit to going all in. Like it or not, the road to success is often filled with stress. Stress associated with success is practically unavoidable. The more successful you become, the more responsibility is placed on you. Ultimately, more success means more stress to manage. As more pressure begins to enter your life, it becomes incredibly important to manage your level of stress by finding a stress reliever. Finding a relief, or as I like to call it "finding your calm," is one of the greatest tools that you can have to combat stress because protecting both your mental and physical health is unequivocally invaluable.

It's important to understand that whenever your balance is off, your level of stress will begin to surge, and things will begin to fall through the cracks; both of which affect your life and work negatively. People with a high level of stress often tend to neglect one of the most important components to their success - their health. Without your health, you are nothing and have nothing. As the old saying goes, "what good is success if you don't live long enough to enjoy it?" No type of work or stress is worth sacrificing your health and well-being.

Self-care is a form of balance and release. Building on the discussion from gem 16, at some point in time, you will need a restful break away from work and others for your mental health. During times of fatigue, listen to your body earnestly. Working endlessly and overexerting yourself is incredibly dangerous. Just like in sports, resting is equally as important as working hard and training. Without proper rest, you will not have the proper recovery you need to grow and progress. Micheal Jordan was known to take frequent golf breaks to get his mind off basketball. Bob Marley played soccer to give his vocal cords a break. The point is, if you want to be a high-functioning successful individual, you must find balance in your life to incorporate the things that bring you calm. Find your calm, use it to lower your stress level, and incorporate it into your life as frequently as you need to. Never let anyone or anything get in the way of your calm, never!

Most forms of stress in our lives can be eliminated or controlled. Recall that your reality is a universal projection of your internal beliefs, understandings, and desires. Knowing this, keeping your vibration high is not only a form of internal alignment, calibration, and protection that helps you to be more in tune with yourself, God, and nature, but is also a way to prevent, mitigate, and remove stress from your life.

Find your calm is your twentieth gem! Having calm in your life is a necessity. When times are stressful, sit yourself down on a mental, spiritual, emotional, and physical charging station. Delve into the things that you love often and remember that life is meant to be an enjoyable experience, not a stressful one. Use your calm to stay in perfect alignment with your purpose and use it to maximize and sustain balance and harmony in your life.

NOTES

NOTES

21

GRATITUDE

"Give thanks for
what you have.
Give effort for
what you want."

Gratitude is the quality of being thankful for your life, opportunities, and experiences. It is another simple, yet powerful tool that can significantly enhance your overall life and well-being. Gratitude is not only a positive state of being, but also a path to internal peace and prosperity. Those who practice gratitude have a certain appreciation and fullness of life, while those who lack gratitude have shallow perspectives and a limited understanding. This is because a lack of gratitude is more than just the absence of thankfulness; it is in greater depth, also a lack of humility and understanding of your purpose.

Having gratitude is a sign of wisdom, maturity, humility, kindness, and high vibration. Through gratitude, you can humbly appreciate every moment and aspect of your existence. Gratitude reminds us that life is truly a gift and that every moment is precious. It is of course easy to show gratitude when times are good and when things are working in your favor. However, practicing gratitude when things aren't going your way is the key to immense growth, change, and fulfillment. During challenging moments, it's very important to remain thankful for what you have and for life in general. If you never learn to be thankful for what you have, you will forever succumb to the illusion of not having enough. Remember that tough times don't last, only tough people do. Be grateful that every second of your life is an opportunity to learn, advance, and move closer to your purpose. Even in the times when things "appear" to be going better for others around you, never make the mistake of comparing your life with theirs. Always stay in your lane and trust that you are right where you are supposed to be. Be grateful for your life and the beauty of it. Once you begin to appreciate and celebrate how far you've come in life, you will adopt greater gratitude for where you are going.

Practicing gratitude helps you to attract major favor and abundance in your life. If you want to acquire more, give thanks first for what you already have (the universe will then manifest more in your life for you to be thankful for). While there are many ways to express gratitude in your life, giving onto others is one of the easiest, most powerful, and effective ways. Whether it's time, money, or energy, giving is a selfless and kind act that shows not only that you care for others, but also that you are thankful for what you have. Always remember what goes around comes around (if you give, so shall you receive).

Gratitude is your twenty-first gem! Without gratitude, it is impossible to truly value anything. Be grateful for your life and show appreciation for it in all that you do. Focus less on what you don't have and more on what you do have. Stay focused and humble and appreciate the journey to becoming a higher version of yourself.

NOTES

NOTES

22

EGO

"Watch your ego, or watch your downfall."

The word ego often has negative connotations associated with it, such as arrogance. However, having an ego isn't necessarily a bad thing. First, understand that your ego is directly connected to your sense of self-worth. As it also relates to your self-esteem, having a healthy ego can be extremely beneficial for your continued healthy sense of self, growth, success, and advancement. In fact, I would argue that ego is a necessary component for greatness. As good as having an ego can be, the problem however arises when your ego is not controlled or becomes in some way imbalanced (the unhealthy form). If not controlled, your ego could also be the very thing that negatively impacts your life and prevents you from reaching success. For this reason, it is crucial for you to always regulate your ego to prevent your own downfall.

Your ego is always present, both when times are good and bad. When times are good, it's important to continue to use your ego to think highly of yourself and to show up confidently in your pursuits. However, it's also important to remain cautious of becoming excessively confident or self-centered (ego used in the wrong way) during these times. When times are bad, don't allow your ego to be consumed with negative associations or emotions such as anger, arrogance, envy, pridefulness, or entitlement. Understand that harboring this type of negative thinking and energy is destructive because it always hinders your success further by trapping you in a perpetual cycle of low vibration.

In my opinion, it is harder (and more important) to watch your ego when times are going well because those are the times when God tests you the most. When times are good, and success is prevalent, becoming egotistical (another negative connotation of ego) is a costly mistake that is far too easy to make, and one that far too many people regret. This is because they are usually humbled, often at the expense of losing the very thing that was the root of their inflated ego.

Watch your ego is your twenty-second gem! To avoid self-sabotage, your ego must always be controlled. Never allow yourself to have an inflated or exaggerated view of yourself. Remember that arrogance is, and will always be, one of your worst enemies. Become great but never forget the source of your greatness. Focus on using your ego to your advantage instead of making it an unnecessary disadvantage in your life. Control your thoughts, actions, and ego at all costs and at all times.

NOTES

NOTES

23

RISE ABOVE
HATE

"Use hate as fuel
for your success
and greatness."

Hate exists in two different forms in our lives, both of which stem from extremely low vibrational thought processes. Either you are the recipient of hatred from others, or you yourself are the culprit. Understanding hate on the receiving end is important because it's outside of your control. No matter how hard you try, or how righteous and kind you are, you will never please everyone. Being disliked or hated by others is completely normal and unavoidable, especially for those who live in their purpose. Like it or not, there will always be at least one person who dislikes you for one reason or another. Sometimes, people who dislike you do nothing more than try to avoid being around you. However, people are sometimes more deliberate and dangerous in their methods of trying to block your shine by maliciously attacking you. Learning how to deal with these types of people in your life is key to protecting yourself and maintaining your peace.

The first step in learning how to deal with being hated is understanding that people will choose to hate you for different reasons (of which some will make entirely no sense). Although the reasons can vary, they all share two common traits: people foolishly hate what they don't understand or what they can't control. People may hate you for growing and changing. They may hate you for dreaming. They may hate you because you did what they couldn't do. They may hate you because of the color of your skin. They may even hate you for smiling and being happy. There are no shortages of reasons. The point is, people will find a reason to hate you if they really want to. Again, no one is immune to experiencing hate. Knowing this, it's important not to take any of the hate you receive personally or let it affect you negatively in any way (especially since people who hate you or hate on you are oftentimes the most like you and secretly your biggest fan). Most people who hate you really don't hate you at all (especially when you have done no wrong). They rather (and ironically) hate an aspect of themselves. Sadly, they are filled with hatred because they are so unhappy with themselves that they attempt to project their internal feelings of misery, suffering, and disappointment onto you to try to make themselves feel better. They only think that they hate you (which is an obvious illusion to a conscious, spiritual, and high-vibrational person) because your spirit most likely irritates their bruised ego and reminds them of their inner insecurities. What's even more frustrating for them is that no matter how hard they try to hate on you, knock you down, or stop your blessings, they eventually realize that their attempts are futile because they can't stop the God in you; and you better believe they will hate you for that too.

The next step in dealing with hate is to simply stay focused on your dreams. Trust that your success will always speak louder than any nonsense your haters could spew. Try as they might, never allow your haters to use their negative energy to bring you outside of your character and down to their lower plane of existence (which is their goal). Remember that the moment you give into their plan and entertain their hatred, you lose. Instead, avoid the traps that they set and continue to work hard to become better each day. As your success continues to increase, so too should your strength and tolerance for haters (as your number of haters will inevitably rise). At a certain point, it also becomes exceedingly wise to use discernment for your personal safety. Be wise and keep your friends and enemies close, as they both are equally capable of causing harm to you. More importantly, never underestimate either of the two.

Lastly, if you're ever guilty of projecting hate onto someone else, it's because you're operating in a low-vibrational state and have lost control over your thoughts, emotions, and ego. Through honest reflection, you will notice that your issue most likely had nothing to do with the other person, but rather your own internal conflict. Through reflection, you will also understand that hate, in any form, is a waste of thought and energy and that you only set yourself up for failure and suffering when you attempt to project it onto others and block their blessings.

Rise above the hate is your twenty-third gem! Remember that how you respond to and handle hatred is a reflection of your character. Being hated on should do nothing more than spark a fire inside of you to become better every day and continue working hard on your dreams. It should not pull you out of your character or cause you to spiral in any way. Having haters is only a testament of the power you have and evidence that others are intimidated by it. When dealing with haters, keep your composure, mind your mind, mind your character, and smile knowing that they are only hating because they also see your greatness. Never allow yourself to hate or hate on anyone. Hating another person is an act of hating yourself. Worst, hating on another person means that you don't fully trust the will and plan that God has for you. Never lose your way trying to prevent others from walking along theirs. Remember that we all have a unique calling and that there is an infinite abundance of blessings and resources for us all. Love is always the way, never hate.

NOTES

NOTES

24

WISDOM

"Walk towards the
light of wisdom."

Wisdom can be abundantly obtained and used to operate at infinitely higher levels of consciousness. It is undoubtedly one of the greatest and most powerful things that you can acquire in your life. Wisdom not only empowers you with truth and understanding but also provides you with an invaluable mental and spiritual compass that guides and protects your footsteps. Being blessed with wisdom is a major advantage in your life that helps you to manifest your dreams and to secure infinite blessings, favor, and protection. Like freshwater on our planet, having wisdom likewise sustains you by nourishing your mind, body, and soul. For this reason, you should always aspire to acquire as much wisdom as you can to apply across all facets of your life.

Wisdom is obtained through two different ways: through personal knowledge and experience or through direct connection to God. The wisdom that you obtain on your own accord comes from your collection, interpretation, and understanding of past experiences (acting on your knowledge). This type of wisdom is acquired both consciously and subconsciously. Gaining wisdom through lived experiences takes maturity, perseverance, and patience. The type of wisdom that you obtain through your direct connection to God requires awareness, stillness, submission, listening, humility, discernment, and obedience. This type of wisdom is pure and divine (extending and manifesting in some capacities beyond your limited human understanding) and continues to increase the more you ascend to greater planes of being and existence (the continuous strive to reach your higher self).

Wisdom may be difficult for some to obtain, but easy to recognize by most. This is because wise people vibrate at higher levels of being and understanding, while sharing similar traits and behavioral patterns. For example, wise people know when to speak and when to remain silent (again, connecting back to gem 16). They know that words are manifestations of thoughts and that thoughts have immense power. They also understand that the tongue is the sacred keeper of life and death.

Another easily recognizable trait of a wise person is humility. Humility requires an incredible amount of self-awareness and is undoubtedly another sign of a high-vibrational person. Humble people are known to be modest, use great discernment, practice restraint and reservation, and to have control over their thoughts, actions, emotions, and ego. Being humble is knowing that there is always something more to learn and understanding that you know nothing at all in the context of the grand and infinite universe. When you are truly humble, you recognize that you are always in a constant state of growing and remain completely open to receiving new information and guidance. Humble people draw strength from their humility and use it to empower others.

Wisdom comes with an innate and arbitrary pressure to remove anything from your life that serves no purpose or that could potentially harm your growth and trajectory. As a rule, anything that is not helping you to become better, helping others to become better, or that carries a low-vibrational energy needs to be immediately removed from your life. This act of purging is one of the most important, beneficial, and terrifying things that you could ever do. Fear not! You must learn to become comfortable listening to the voice of wisdom, no matter what it asks of you. Never let the fear of outgrowing people, places, or things prevent you from receiving your blessing. One of the worst things that you could ever do is hold yourself back to please others out of fear of leaving them behind. Have comfort in knowing that wisdom will always protect and push you in the direction of truth, sound decisions, elevation, and advancement.

Despite its massive importance in our lives, few are willing (and have the patience) to actively seek wisdom or go through the process to receive it. As a result, those who are wise are consequently charged with (possibly burdened with) leading the growth and expansion of our world. As beautiful and rewarding as it is to acquire more knowledge and wisdom, doing so comes with a price (as all things do). The price is sacrificing your time, energy, love, relationships, and desires while you go through (often simultaneously) a period of loneliness, frustration, defeat, misunderstanding, and hatred from others. Knowing this, and that wisdom holds each person who receives it to a higher standard, accountability, and responsibility, it is very important to be mindful of what you ask God for. If you truly think that you are ready to receive more wisdom, make sure that you are also truly ready to make the necessary life-changing sacrifices and adjustments to receive it first. As a rule, never ask for anything that you're not ready to receive and remember that each level you climb will require a higher version of yourself. Embrace the change (nothing changes if nothing changes) and be ready to leave certain things behind.

Wisdom is your twenty-fourth gem, and what I like to call a super gem because it is essentially all your previous gems combined into one! Wisdom is infinite. Wisdom is God. And wisdom is eternally you, an extension of the infinite wisdom of God. Wisdom will lead you to higher levels of being and understanding. Remember that it doesn't matter how much you know, but rather what you choose to do with the knowledge that you have. Seek and obtain wisdom, then share it with anyone who is willing to listen and ready to receive it. Use your wisdom for growth, understanding, discernment, and guidance. Most importantly, be wise and use your knowledge for good and righteousness - as any other reason really wouldn't be wise at all.

NOTES

NOTES

25

BOSS UP

"There are no shortcuts
to greatness."

When it comes to manifesting your goals, your only focus should be working as hard as you can and bossing up until you reach success. If you've never heard the expression before, "boss up" is a saying that essentially means doing something to the fullest, taking charge of your future, and handling your business by any means. Bossing up is a mentality that involves putting in major work, outworking your competition, breaking barriers, raising the bar, making sacrifices, applying pressure, and never making excuses or giving up. It also involves devoting as much time as you can into thinking, planning, and working to turn your dreams into reality. One thing that is certain, bossing up is a behavior that stems from (and reflects) a mentality that is indicative of people who fully believe in themselves, and who also understand the value and importance of determination, consistent hard work, growth, and advancement.

The single best word that ultimately describes what it means to boss up is action. Action is the most important aspect of turning any dream into a reality. Whether you're starting your own business, getting through school, or embarking on some form of self-improvement, nothing gets accomplished without action. Action separates those who will succeed from those who will not. As previously stated, far too many people sit on the sidelines and watch their dreams never happen because they fail to act. To obtain the life that you desire, you must meet God halfway by taking the first step towards your goals. Once you take action in your life, so will He. Taking the first step is extremely powerful because it shows God not only that you are obedient and have faith, but also that you are serious about manifesting your goals.

In greater detail, bossing up is about choosing to go above and beyond what is asked, required, or even expected of you. It's about going the extra mile, even after you have already gone the extra mile. For example, if you're exercising and your trainer asks you to do one more rep, shoot to give him five more. If you only have one day left on your diet, push yourself and go another week. Or, if you usually only work 30 minutes a day on your personal goals, start making it a habit to put in at least an hour of work every day. This is what bossing up means; pushing yourself further and further to reach greatness, even (and especially) when no one else is watching. Yes, it's difficult, but bossing up is not about taking the easy road. Bossing up is about taking action to achieve success.

Again, if you were honest with yourself, you would probably admit that you aren't working nearly as hard as you could be towards your goals. Stop wasting time and prolonging your blessings. By now, you already know what you need to do. Boss up, hustle, and get it done. It's that simple. In fact, it's so simple that most people find it difficult. Don't be like most people. Get to work and remain serious about your purpose and future. Unless you intentionally devote the time to working on your goals, you will unfortunately find that accomplishing them will always seem to evade you (or, at the very least prove to be extremely challenging). Change your mentality and habits for the better and start making it a habit to boss up for your dreams every day.

Bossing up will mean nothing to an ordinary person, yet everything to an extraordinary person. Although bossing up admittedly comes with a lot of pressure, so too does a life of regret. Start using the pressure of becoming who you are meant to be to your advantage and working like your goals are the only things that are keeping you alive. You know that you are bossing up and being serious about your future if your goals are keeping you up late at night or waking you up early in the morning. Step up to the plate and make the necessary sacrifices. The sooner you act, the sooner you will be blessed. Make sure that you are putting in work every day until you accomplish your goals, and even then, celebrate the moment, then hop right back on the grind towards the next goal. That's the secret to success, realizing that there are no shortcuts and staying hungry for more.

Boss up is your twenty-fifth and final gem! Your life is too important and your purpose too meaningful for you to procrastinate. Stop talking, start acting, and fulfill your destiny. Press the gas and boss up every day to turn your dreams into reality. If you aren't going to boss up for your dreams, who will? Boss up for yourself. Boss up for your loved ones. Boss up for God. Boss up for the world!

NOTES

NOTES

PART III END

Knowing how to effectively approach your goals and having the self-discipline to work until all your goals are accomplished are two extremely valuable skills that you must possess to elevate your life. Moreover, knowing how to sustain the accomplishments that you earn, while being able to effectively handle the complexities of success, are two particularly invaluable skills that must be learned, developed, and mastered to grow and expand your success. For this reason, Part III of this book was strategically written to not only give insight into how to manage success, but also to provide knowledge and awareness on how to take care of yourself (all aspects of your mental, physical, spiritual, and emotional self) during successful times. Whether it's learning how to remain humble and motivated, or remembering the importance of rest and healing, the gems in Part III of this book harmoniously provide a source of wisdom on how to effectively deal with the inevitable challenges of accomplishing your goals and the demands of success. Furthermore, Part III is titled Reaching & Keeping Success (The Crown) because it depicts the full external manifestation of your internal vision through your will, purpose, intentions, and implementations.

The crown, in its essence, represents your season of manifestation, growth, expansion, and reaping the fruits of your labor. Much like the characteristics of a tree, the crown of your journey will only manifest if and only if your foundation (in this context, consisting of both The Root and The Trunk) is strong and healthy and over the course of time, patience, consistency, hard work, and growth. Reaching this stage of your journey is incredibly rewarding, not only because you get to reap the fruits of all the hard work, patience, and faith that you exhibited in yourself and your purpose, but also because it simultaneously rewards you with a deep sense of pride and fulfillment.

It is also very important to understand that all the relationships, connections, and support systems that you form along your journey are extensions of your vision and are the metaphoric branches of your crown. Making high-vibrational connections is critical because they ultimately play a pivotal role in the overall health, vitality, and viability of your success. Therefore, as your success (crown) continues to grow, so too should the strength and support of your branches.

Also in similar form to a tree, in order to have and sustain a healthy crown, you must constantly absorb positive energy (light), filter out negative and harmful entities, and protect your flourishing manifestation from the threats of your surrounding environment at all costs. In doing so, be sure to remove any dead or dying leaves (lower-vibrational energies) from your crown as quickly as possible so that they don't negatively siphon energy from your thriving tree of success (including depleting the health of yourself). This necessary process of pruning your crown is an effective way of managing yourself and your success and will undoubtedly encourage new growth, opportunity, and fruitfulness in your life.

Lastly, remember that a thriving crown stems from a tree that is healthy and able to adapt to its environment. If you are unable to adapt to your surroundings or endure the storms and challenges that you will inevitably experience, your success will diminish and eventually perish. In moments of difficulty, remember that the strongest people always endure the toughest battles, and that the greater the battle, the sweeter the crown. In times of fatigue, remember that recharging is massively important and should be a requirement in your life. In times of success, remember to stay humble and sharp because there will always be more things to learn, areas to improve on, and infinitely more levels to climb.

THE POWER
OF THE
TONGUE

"Seek it. Speak it. See it."

One of the best things that you can do for yourself and your future is to start applying the 25 gems presented in this book to your everyday life. This is because collectively, the gems provide an abundance of truth, perspective, wisdom, guidance, inspiration, and motivation to help you successfully master yourself and your purpose and will lead you on a path of greatness and fulfillment. The best way to adapt all the gems into your life is to start becoming one with them. This means intentionally integrating the concepts and teachings of the gems in as many different areas of your life as possible. For example, affirmations are known to be very powerful and effective at attracting and manifesting things into your life. Affirmations are so effective because they are powerful statements, intentionally spoken out loud, that are intended to positively affect the conscious and subconscious mind by aiming to eliminate negative thoughts, emotions, and behaviors. As such, the practice of saying affirmations out loud, especially daily, can consequentially become an act of speaking things into existence and can be used as a powerful and effective way to regularly incorporate the gems of this book into your life.

Affirmations are also the perfect way to show that you have faith and trust in the power of the tongue and the law of attraction. Getting into the habit of saying affirmations daily is highly beneficial because it places your mind (both the conscious and subconscious) in a constant state of thinking about, believing in, and attracting the things that you desire into your life. The repetitiveness of saying affirmations daily can also completely transform your life because it can lead to increased accomplishments and shorter manifestation times. This simply means the more frequently you use affirmations to speak things into existence, the more your mind believes what your mouth is saying (on both a spiritual and cellular level) and the faster it works to make what you are saying a reality.

AFFIRMATIONS

"Speak power over your life."

The 25 gems of this book have been conveniently incorporated into three different affirmations sets (morning, afternoon, and evening) for your daily practice. The morning affirmation set was designed to set the rhythm of the day, the afternoon affirmation set to elevate your frequency and restore the mind's focus, and the evening affirmation set to allow you to end your day on a positive, productive, and high-vibrational note towards manifesting your goals. Since affirmations are meant to be tailored specifically for you, it is recommended that you use the following affirmations as a template to get you started, and if necessary, adjust them to meet your own personal goals and intentions. It is still, however, strongly recommend that you in some way incorporate the gems of this book into your affirmations to achieve more understanding, growth, advancement, manifestation, and sustainability in your life.

Affirmations Set #1 (Morning)

I am a powerful, righteous being with divine clarity and anointing.

I am eternally blessed and destined for greatness.

I have a strong **MENTALITY** to succeed and will always push myself to become better through hard work and patience.

I will give nothing less than my best effort at all times and accept nothing less than growth and improvement.

I choose to walk in truth, righteousness, and light and to not let anything or anyone deter me from the sanctity of my beliefs, dreams, and moralities.

I have the power to change my **ENVIRONMENT** for the better and will always aim to be a positive influence to those around me.

I have the **CONFIDENCE** to accomplish anything that I desire and the faith, courage, and patience to see all things through.

I have tremendous **VISION** over my life and full control over my thoughts and actions.

I will always think positively of myself and twice before I speak or act because I know the power that my words and actions hold.

I vow to **MASTER MY MIND** so that I can master my life.

I choose love, peace, positivity, respect, strength, intelligence, and discernment in all that I do.

In this moment, I choose to give thanks for all that I have and to release and rebuke all negativity from my life.

Everything that I need to accomplish my goals and to create the life that I want is already being attracted to me through powerful forms of **MAGNETISM.**

I live and walk in **PURPOSE** because my purpose is my obligation.

I know that my life is necessary and that it was manifested with divine intelligence and intention.

I walk with faith, never **FEAR**, because I understand the calling over my life and my connection to God.

No matter my current **CIRCUMSTANCE**, I am certain that greatness lies within me and my future.

Affirmations Set #2 (Afternoon)

I am present, blessed, grateful, humble, and thankful for life.

I have understanding and **PATIENCE** that the universe is making a way for me to succeed.

Even in times of adversity, I have no reason to worry because everything is working in my favor.

I am strong enough to handle any **PRESSURE** that life brings and brave enough to live fearlessly.

Through vision, hard work, and **CONSISTENCY**, I know that I can manifest anything that I desire.

I am thankful for the abundance of love, peace, and prosperity in my life and will always try to use my blessings to uplift others.

My spirit is strong, pure, righteous, and eternally powerful.

I am forever blessed in all aspects of my existence - past, present, and future.

In this moment, I claim and attract high-vibrational energy in all areas of my life.

I have the **DISCIPLINE** to be great and the love for myself and others to be humble and obedient.

I will always choose to **BET ON MYSELF** in any and every way possible.

I completely **TRUST THE PROCESS** God has for my life.

I am not afraid to use the power of **SILENCE** to hear the answers I seek or heal the wounds I carry.

No matter what, I refuse to fear the unknown.

I have all that I need because the infinite and divine **HIGHER POWER** is guiding and protecting me always, in all ways.

I will always **REMEMBER THE WHY** of my purpose and existence and never neglect or forsake it.

Affirmations Set #3 (Evening)

I am the master of my actions, sole protector of my legacy, guardian of my internal peace, and affirmation of truth and righteousness.

I humbly accept the privilege, power, and purpose of my life and will **KEEP WORKING** hard to become the person I am destined to be.

I am both ready and open to receive more intelligence, enlightenment, and direction from God.

I will receive more blessings because I am calm, centered, and in perfect harmony with God and the universe.

I am blessed because I have balance in my life, sincerity in my intentions, and selflessness in my actions.

I will always **FIND MY CALM** so that I am healthy, balanced, and able to pursue my purpose.

My life is, and will always be, positively filled with the spirit of love, humility, giving, and respect.

I have tremendous **GRATITUDE** for who I am, all that I have, and everything that I've overcome.

I trust that I am exactly where I need to be in this moment, and that my obedience will make a way for my purpose.

I understand both the strength and weakness of **EGO** and will always do my best to use it as strength.

I choose to **RISE ABOVE HATE** because I know those who are filled with hatred never experience the gift of love.

I welcome, claim, and receive higher vibrations, consciousness, favor, understanding, and peace in all areas of my life.

I am capable of attracting higher levels of mental, spiritual, physical, emotional, and financial planes of existence.

I am blessed to have an abundance of **WISDOM**, resources, and protection to guide me along my path to success and enlightenment.

No matter the circumstance, I will always work hard and never give up on my dreams.

I will **BOSS UP** for God, myself, my loved ones, and the world.

I know that I am righteous.

I know that I am great.

I know that I will succeed.

I AM powerful beyond measure.

I AM the manifestation of pure love and light.

WRITE YOUR OWN AFFIRMATIONS

_____

_____

_____

_____

_____

_____

_____

_____

_____

_____

_____

_____

_____

_____

_____

_____

_____

_____

_____

_____

_____

_____

_____

_____

_____

_____

_____

WRITE YOUR OWN AFFIRMATIONS

WRITE YOUR OWN AFFIRMATIONS

_____
_____
_____
_____
_____
_____
_____
_____
_____
_____
_____
_____
_____
_____
_____
_____
_____
_____
_____
_____
_____
_____
_____
_____

WRITE YOUR OWN AFFIRMATIONS

_____

_____

_____

_____

_____

_____

_____

_____

_____

_____

_____

_____

_____

_____

_____

_____

_____

_____

_____

_____

_____

_____

_____

_____

_____

_____

_____

_____

_____

_____

PLAN IT OUT

"The life you want is only a plan away."

WRITE YOUR PLAN

Who are you?

_____

_____

What is your God given purpose?

_____

_____

What goal would you like to accomplish?

_____

_____

Why do you want to accomplish this goal?

_____

_____

How does this goal align with your purpose?

_____

_____

How does this goal align with your short and long-term plans?

_____

_____

When do you want to accomplish this goal by?

_____

_____

_____

When will you start working on this goal?

_____

_____

What do you need to accomplish this goal? Do you currently have
what you need? If not, how and when will you get what you need
to accomplish this goal?

_____

_____

What action will you take to accomplish this goal?

_____

_____

How will you hold yourself accountable to make sure that you
stay on track to accomplish this goal by your desired date? What
will you do if you don't accomplish it by your desired date?

_____

_____

_____

Where do you see yourself in the next year? 3yrs? 5yrs? 10yrs?

_____

_____

_____

_____

_____

WRITE YOUR PLAN

_____
_____
_____
_____
_____
_____
_____
_____
_____
_____
_____
_____
_____
_____
_____
_____
_____
_____
_____
_____
_____
_____
_____
_____
_____
_____

WRITE YOUR PLAN

_____
_____
_____
_____
_____
_____
_____
_____
_____
_____
_____
_____
_____
_____
_____
_____
_____
_____
_____
_____
_____
_____
_____
_____
_____
_____
_____
_____

SUMMARY & CONCLUSION

"Become
THE BETTER YOU
so that nothing can
get in the way of
your happiness
and success."

Congratulations on completing this book and taking a huge step towards becoming a better you and achieving the life that you want and deserve! You now have a better understanding of what it takes to manifest your goals, achieve greatness, sustain your success, and push for future growth and advancement. This book is divided into three parts which cover the three stages of manifestation and success - Part I: The Foundation of Manifestation & Success (The Roots), Part II: Working Towards Manifestation & Success (The Trunk), and Part III: Reaching & Keeping Success (The Crown). The 25 gems contained in this book will help you become the best version of yourself, change your life for the better, and accomplish the goals that you desire.

Part I of this book teaches you to have a strong mentality, a positive and supportive environment, great confidence and vision, the ability to master your mind, and an understanding of the laws of magnetism to accomplish your goals and manifest greatness. It also teaches you to build your life around your purpose, have no fear, and bounce back quickly from setbacks and unfortunate circumstances. The gems presented in Part I are integral to your future success because they are the core foundations for both your internal and external growth and advancement.

Part II focuses on expanding on your foundational knowledge from Part I and laying down the groundwork for your future success. The gems in Part II teach that you need patience, to be able to handle pressure, and to have extreme consistency and discipline to fully manifest your goals. It also covers the importance of betting on yourself, trusting the process, understanding and using the power of silence to your benefit, connecting to The Higher Power, and remembering your why on your path.

Part III of this book focuses on the season of reaping the benefits of all your hard work and sacrifices. The gems in Part III show you how to remain balanced while experiencing success, keep and sustain your accomplishments, and avoid the detriment of complacency. Part III teaches that the way to sustain your success is rooted in pushing yourself to new heights, working hard, having proper balance in life, and showing immense gratitude for the blessings that you already have. It also covers the importance of controlling your ego, rising above any hate you may receive, and seeking life-long wisdom. Part III concludes with the last gem of the book - boss up every day so that you can accomplish your goals and make your dreams a reality.

Now that you have the gems to create the life that you want, the only thing left for you to do is to make it happen. Although it's a massive test of your faith, the truth is that chasing greatness is one of the most beautiful, rewarding, and priceless experiences that you will ever have. Bury your excuses, learn as much as you can, use your gems, and do your best to uplift yourself and others in the process. No matter how many things you accomplish, or how successful you become, remain humble and focused and never become complacent. Align yourself to your purpose, stay positive and righteous, and never become discouraged or give up. Be patient as sometimes your blessing may take months or even years to appear. Trust in your timing, intuition, and the divine calling over your life. Be grateful and remember that the power to change your life lies within your own mind and hands. Give thanks to God, boss up, and get to work on becoming a better you!

Congratulations on your future success and happiness! I look forward to seeing the positive impact you have on our world.

Love, Peace, & Blessings,
Steven Berryhill Jr., Ph.D

"A better you today
means a better life
for you tomorrow."

ABOUT THE AUTHOR

Dr. Steven Berryhill Jr. grew up in Stone Mountain, Georgia. He is an educator, consultant, speaker, and truth seeker. Passionate about education and advancement, his writing focuses on helping people develop the mentality, tools, confidence, and habits that lead to deep personal growth, increased goal accomplishment and success, and personal greatness.

He received his Ph.D. in Urban Higher Education from Jackson State University, and both his Master's in Environmental Engineering and Bachelor's in Mathematics from Tennessee State University. His higher education experience spans across several leadership, administration, and teaching roles and includes involvement in numerous education boards, programs, and community service and outreach organizations.

Dr. Berryhill travels around the country motivating people and organizations to reach their full potential by helping them to develop the skills and practices that lead to long-term improvement and success. As an advocate of education and development, Dr. Berryhill founded his company SBJ LEADERSHIP, LLC in 2024. His platform provides a variety of educational services such as professional development, consultation, workshops, training, education advocacy, and curriculum and policy development for educators, students, and organizations.

Contact:

- Steven Berryhill Jr.
- drstevenberryhill
- dr_berryhill
- linkedin.com/in/steven-berryhill-jr
- www.sbjleadership.com

Made in the USA
Columbia, SC
04 January 2025

51118895R00113